Y0-BYA-389

Published by: TAG Books
PO Box 111
Independence OR 97351

Distributor: Wade Martin's Bonanza Distribution

Cover Design and Artwork by Sheila Somerville. The artist may be contacted by writing to TAG Books.

Copyright 1996 - Gary D. Trump
Printed in the United States - First Edition

ISBN: 1-884366-02-3

Other books in the Uncle Bud series:

I Remember When
Sweet Memories
Lookin' Back

Well hi there! Good to see you again. Y'know, you've been stoppin' by enough now that we've decided to make you a full-fledged member of the group.

See that shelf there on the back wall? The one with all the coffee cups? We had your name stenciled on a cup, and it's right there on the end. Now you've got your own cup, and that's good, but then if the waitresses are busy and you need a refill, you're expected to get your own. Of course, that's why we shove a couple of tables together here at the end of the counter ... so it isn't so far to the coffee pot ... and that's good.

On the other hand, you're sittin' with all the old duffers and duffettes that inhabit this place. Still, you're now considered a member of the family, and that's good. Now, I'll admit that it's a pretty strange family, so you can get up and walk out any time you feel like it, and that's good ... but we'll talk about you when you're gone.

We got on the subject of cosmetics the other day and talkin' about how some gals seem to think that if one coat is fine, then three or four layers must be even better.

Then we got around to how expensive the stuff is and finally Pete said, "Well, all I know

1

is that Gladys spent fifty dollars on one of those mud pack outfits."

"Did it make her prettier?" Joe asked.

"Yeah, for a while, it did," nodded Pete, "but then all the mud fell off."

Remember how much fun you had when the circus came to town? They're pretty much gone now. It's a shame too, because they were great entertainment. Fortunately, we'll always have Congress.

Okay, so maybe I don't make the world's greatest cup of coffee. But I notice that every morning Tom fills a cup and takes it with him. The other day he made another crack about the coffee, so I called him on it.

"I do it as a public service," Tom explained.

"So there'll be less for other people to drink, I suppose."

"Nope. Every morning when I drive up behind the store, there's a band of pygmies waitin' to dip their arrows in it."

This last year, Martha took up couponing. She takes advantage of every store sale. Says she's stocking up ... just in case. Gives me a warm feelin' to know our son Curt will have enough shaving lotion for his great grandkids.

Nobody can imagine what the end of the world will be like: The terror, the agony, the cries of misery and pain ... unless you've been the parent of a 16 year-old girl who still doesn't have a date two weeks before the prom.

The difference between a guest and a pest is about three days.

It's been years ago now, but folks still talk about Jasper Hanks from time to time. Jasper was a part-time farmer, part-time gambler, and full-time character. Rough as a cob, too.

Just yesterday I was tellin' Doc Guthrie about ol' Doc Krebbs and the time Jasper showed up at his office.

"Doc," Jasper says, "when you get time would you mind stoppin' by my place and takin' a bullet out of my son-in-law's leg?"

"What?" Doc says. "Your son-in-law's been shot?"

"Yep," Jasper nods.

"Who shot him?"

"I reckon I did."

3

"Jasper! You shot your own son-in-law?"

"Well, he wasn't my son-in-law at the time."

I've heard that Oliver Wendell Holmes, Jr., once said to a lawyer, "This is a court of law, young man, not a court of justice." Well, I think that most of us would agree that truth and justice go hand in hand, so the unspoken part of that statement is as important as what was said.

We were all sittin' around havin' coffee the other morning and we got to talkin' about all the different charities. It seems like you can't turn around without being hit up for a donation by one outfit or the next, all of them thinkin' that they're more deserving than any of the others. I guess that, in a way, it just goes to show how old we are. We can all remember when charity was a personal kindness before it became a business.

There's a pretty happy group workin' here, and I'm not shy in tellin' people about it. But the other day Jean grabbed me by the elbow and said, "Listen, Bud. While you're back there at the grill, I have to deal with the public and a couple of college kids working their first real job. Every morning I have to deal with you and four other old geezers who drink coffee and razz me to death for a half an hour before we open. So if you insist on telling folks I'm a 'gruntled employee' you may as well add a 'dis' in front of it."

Nice woman. No sense of humor, though.

Joe's dad was a trader, you know, and Joe got the habit from him. When him and Marge bought their house, it was a nice place. But Joe kept haulin' home bargains he'd picked up at auctions and secondhand stores and what not. Pretty soon, the yard was covered with tools and equipment, and posts and pipe, and just about anything you can imagine. The garage was crammed full of stuff that Joe had found here and there until finally he couldn't get the door closed.

In the end, the city fathers got together and told Joe if he was gonna have a junk yard, then he had to build an eight foot fence around it.

Joe was outraged. "That's not junk," he said. "That's all good stuff."

Well, about that time, Marge weighed in with her opinion, which went something like this: "Listen, you, I've never been able to raise a flower or a vegetable without you piling junk on it. Either that junk goes or you do."

Well, Joe didn't like it, but he finally started loadin' up his old pickup. He hauled stuff to the junk yard, secondhand stores, and city dump for about two weeks. His last trip was into the city's scrap metal dealer. On the way back, he passed an auction.

Marge had just finished puttin' in her new rose garden when he hauled in the first load of new junk. She threw down her shovel and came down to the cafe for a cup of coffee. "Well," she said, "what can I do? I love him. And it's a good thing, too, or I'd have poisoned him years ago."

"I'm an optimist." Gladys says. "Being married to him," she nods at Pete, "I've had to be."

"You're like every other optimist," grins Pete. "You say you are, but you still look both ways when you cross a one-way street."

Marriages may be made in heaven, but all the work is goin' on down here.

Tom has owned his sporting goods and hardware store for a good many years now. Before that he was, in his words, "climbin' the corporate ladder."

"Well," says Tom, "I went to climbin' that ladder and I got part way up. One day I looked down, and I saw all those eager, aggressive faces lookin' up at me. Then I glanced up. I saw what you'd expect to see of people above you on a ladder. Well, I got to thinkin' about it and I quit. Then I went out and bought my own ladder."

We were talkin' about Republicans and Democrats gettin' together on a particular issue the other day when Joe says, "Well, politics makes strange bedfellows."

"What about sports?" Pete asks. "Talk about strange bedfellows."

"Don't forget about big corporations," Tom adds. "They've got their share."

Luther had been takin' all this in and finally he tugged his cap down and eyed each of us in turn. "Listen," he growled, "everything you just mentioned is heavy on lawyers, and a lawyer will go to bed with anybody."

Considering that Luther was divorced years ago, it seemed a good idea to change the subject.

"Y'know," Luther was sayin' the other day,

"sometimes I can tell exactly what an animal is thinkin'. For example, yesterday I was climbin' up to the barn loft. There's boards nailed across the studs to make a ladder, and when I grabbed one of 'em, it let go and I fell backwards into the hay mow."

"Hurt yourself?" I asked.

"No," Luther laughed with a shake of his head. "I fell onto some baled straw. Shook me up a little, though. Anyhow, I'm layin' there tryin' to get my wind back and old Prince, my cow dog, comes runnin' up to me. He's whinin' and lickin' my face, and you can just tell he's sayin', *Oh my gosh! Are you all right, boss? Are you hurt? Gee, I sure hope not.*"

Luther grinned. "Just then, I spied old Tom, the barn cat, sittin' on top of the stanchions. He's lookin' at me and, as sure as I'm sittin' here, he's sayin', *Damn! If he dies, who's gonna feed me?*"

"When I die," says Pete, "I want to go peacefully in my sleep, like grandpa did ... not screamin' in terror like his passengers."

I think I told you about the trouble we had with Curt when he took up cussin'. Well once Martha got friendly with the Andersons, who

were new in town and had a boy about Curt's age. They were throwin' a birthday party for the kid, and before Martha would agree to let Curt go, she made this lady promise to kick him out if he started cussin'.

On the day of the party, Martha dropped Curt off and drove over to the beauty parlor on main street. She'd hardly had time to sit down when Curt walked in.

"Curt!" she yelled, droppin' her magazine. "I know exactly what you're here for! Mrs. Anderson made you leave the party because you were swearing, didn't she? ... Well? Didn't she?"

Curt kind of pulled his mouth to the side like he does and said, "How the hell could she? You left me at the wrong damn house?"

Anne's been workin' for me for years, and she's often the one who has to show the kids I hire how to do the job. I've seen her stand right there in the middle of the room with her hands on her hips while the kid goes back and recleans every table to her satisfaction. You can bet that if they're here any time at all, they leave believing what she always tells them.

"Take the time to do it right or make the time to do it over."

Y'know, if you hang around here long enough, sooner or later you're bound to run across somebody who tells you he's just a poor, dumb ol' country boy. Now, I'm not sayin' you shouldn't talk to him, but I would suggest you keep a good, firm grip on your billfold while you're doin' it.

"It's all right to make small loans to friends or family members," Martha likes to say. "Just call it a loan when you give it to them, but think of it as a gift. And keep in mind that large loans often make large enemies."

We used to have a fella come in here who didn't seem quite like most of our customers. He was goin' bald on top, but the rest of his hair hung down to the middle of his back. His beard was short and turning gray, but it was well-trimmed. The standard uniform this guy favored was sandals, shorts, and a T-shirt. The shirt always had some political message on it, usually about the environment.

Now, around here, we usually try to cut folks a lot of slack about politics and religion and what not. Besides, we're all concerned about the environment; we just don't all agree on the approach we should take.

Anyhow, this fella would come in once in a

while, usually with a woman who was dressed about the same as he was. They never caused any trouble, and we didn't offer any.

One Saturday this couple came in for lunch with several other people. It was a warm, fall day and the opening of deer hunting season. From their conversation it seemed they had been out running around the woods trying to scare off the deer and bothering the deer hunters as much as they could.

A hunter's camper had been vandalized and, while these folks didn't say they had actually done it, they seemed to know an awful lot about it. They were getting plenty of satisfaction from it all.

Well, it turned out that the hunter whose camper was wrecked was a pretty determined guy. He set up a tent and stayed right where he was. He made it okay that first night, but the second night a black bear tore open the tent and mauled this fella. Put him in the hospital for a couple of weeks.

It was the morning after the attack that these folks came in again, and they were just thrilled. Now attacks on people by black bears are mighty rare, and I mentioned this fact. They told me that it was partly through their efforts that bear and cougar hunting had been cut way back, and it just pointed out that there are more bears than there used to be. I recall wonderin' out loud that maybe these critters no longer had the fear of people that they once did. Anyhow, these folks headed back to the city full of hot cakes and satisfaction.

It was late spring when this fella I was tellin' you about showed up again. He and his lady friend were headed out (so he said) to go backpackin' in the woods. I didn't expect to see either of 'em for several more days, but the lady was back the next morning, and she was pretty upset. Her boyfriend, it seemed, had forgotten his camera and hiked back to the car to get it. He didn't make it back to camp that night. The lady looked for him on her way out the next morning, but when she got to their car and he wasn't there, she drove to town for help.

I made a phone call, and a bunch of local folks who are members of the sheriff's search and rescue team took time off from their jobs and went lookin' for this fella. It took a couple of days, but they found him ... what was left of him. A cougar ate him.

We were all havin' coffee as usual the next mornin' and talkin' it over.

"I think I see what this all boils down to," Pete said, as he stirred his brew.

"What's that?" I asked.

"Well," he nodded, "seems to me that when the meat eaters are hungry, they don't take much notice of the philosophical outlook of the meat."

I'm not sure I'd put it quite that way, but it probably holds true for countries, people or critters.

Tom says that when he and Alice were first married, they just couldn't seem to get by on his paycheck. They decided they needed a budget, so they sat down and made one out.

"That pointed out our major problem," says Tom. "Then we knew we really couldn't get by on my paycheck."

"Remember ol' Bert Shoop, Phil's dad?" Pete asked.

Well, we all did. Ol' Bert was a good guy. He had a lot of ground up in that dry foothill country. He raised wheat mostly, and it was a tough row to hoe there for quite a while. He just was able to scratch out a livin' up until the war came. Then the government stepped in with subsidies and what not and pretty soon ol' Bert was makin' money hand over fist. You'd never know it the way he lived though, and his kids didn't seem to have much more than most others.

"Once," Pete was sayin', "I helped him out when he was shorthanded during harvest.

There was a kid workin' for him, runnin' a combine. His name was Dan Kelly, and he was just out of high school. We'd been workin' ten or twelve days straight, sunup to sundown, and one morning, Dan asked Bert for the day off. Dan had a girlfriend and he wanted to go see her.

No, said Bert. He looked up at the sky which was overcast, and told the kid, *only if it rains. Then you can go 'cause we can't thresh wet wheat anyhow.*

"In those days," Pete went on, "combines weren't self-propelled. We pulled 'em with a crawler tractor. Bert was runnin' the trap wagon (a parts and fuel truck), and while I was gettin' a tank of diesel, he looked over and there's Kelly jumpin' around on the back of the combine."

What's that idiot think he's doin' now? Bert asked.

"A rain dance," I told him. Well, we laughed about it. Kelly was as Irish as Paddy's pig and wouldn't know a rain dance from a waltz. Within an hour it was rainin' cats and dogs.

"About a week later, Dan asked for the day off again. The sky was bright and clear with just a single little tuft of cloud showin' in the whole wild, blue yonder.

"Bert just laughed at him. *No*, he said, *and I don't think your little dance is gonna work for*

15

you today.

"Kelly climbed up on the back of his combine and went to dancin'.

Pete leaned forward and shook his head. "I'm tellin' you for a fact, pretty soon that one, tiny little cloud turned gray and then black, and it started to grow. Inside of an hour the rain was comin' down in buckets, and we all had to quit work while Kelly went off to visit his girlfriend again."

"A few days later, I got to work just before Kelly and was standin' right there when he walked up to ol' Bert and asked for the day off. It was a clear morning with hardly a cloud in the sky, and Bert took a long look at it before he turned to me and said, *I'll be runnin' Kelly's combine while he takes the day off.*"

Luther's havin' a problem findin' somebody to work for him.

"What's goin' on?" he asks. "Is it that we don't have enough work that people want or that we don't have enough people that want to work?"

Jensen claims that Elmer brought his cousin Bill into the bar a while back and bought him a drink. Jensen says he poured

16

them both straight shots of whiskey and Elmer, pro that he is, knocked his back in one gulp. His cousin, though, held his nose and closed his eyes before he picked up his shot glass. Then he tossed it down just like Elmer.

"Not much of a drinker, I see," Jensen says.,

"I wouldn't say that," cousin Bill replies. "It's just that when I see or smell the stuff, my mouth waters so bad it dilutes the booze."

"I know some folks say that spendin' time in the military is good for a young man," Luther nods, "but I can't tell that it did much for me. I will say this though, it taught me that no matter what kind of troubles you might have, no matter how bad things may get, if there ain't nobody shootin' at you, then things could be a whole helluva lot worse."

He was a child of the depression. The youngest in a large family, he watched his parents struggle with all they had to provide food and shelter for their children. The older kids could help out, too, but he was only five and there was little he could do.

There wasn't much to go around, even in the beginning, but then the depression tightened its grip and soon there wasn't even that. Then the bank foreclosed on their small farm, and they had to get out.

His mother made up packs for herself, her husband, and the older children. They would all have to walk. Even the old horse and wagon had been sold in the past few months in a final desperate effort to hang on to the farm.

That last night at home, Clayton knew something was terribly wrong, and he knew it involved him. Everyone was being very nice to him. His brothers and sisters took turns sitting beside him as the packs were being made up. His mother had tears in her eyes and his father wouldn't look at him. Clayton was frightened. So frightened that he only nodded or shook his head when they spoke to him. Frightened enough that he thought if he just sat still and was very, very good, maybe whatever was going to happen wouldn't take place ... if he was just good enough ...

The next morning, they all started down the road, his mother crying as they walked away. Clayton held on to her hand, hurrying to keep up and shaking with grief, but making no noise as the tears ran down his cheeks.

A mile down the road, they turned in at another farm, and somehow, Clayton wasn't surprised when his father knelt beside him and cleared his throat. Clayton swallowed hard and looked at his bare feet. There were some words ... "too little to keep up" ... "long way to go" ... "no money" ... and finally, "the Kerns are good folks. You mind what they say until we can come back for you." Ernie and Bea Kern had come outside, and they stood by as Clayton's family said goodbye.

It was the defining moment of Clayton's life. His mother, tears streaming down her face, picked him up for one last, long hug. "We'll come back for you," she whispered. "I swear we will."

But he knew she wouldn't. In the end, he was just a little boy, standing in a dusty lane, watching the people he loved walk away.

The Kerns were good people, but they had four kids of their own. At first he slept on a pallet on the floor of the boys' room, but he just didn't fit in. When Ernie fixed up a little room in the barn, Clayton was glad to move in, just to get away from the boys. Not that they beat him up or anything ... they just made sure he knew he didn't belong and never would.

As the years went by, Clayton worked long, hard hours on the farm and went to school with the other kids. But after the eighth grade, the Kerns kept him home to work and the hours got longer and harder.

Two years later Clayton showed up at my grandparents place looking for work. Now my

owner, but just as neat and well kept. We had a cup of coffee and Clayton showed me around. We were standing on the porch and up to then Clayton had made no mention of his wife. And then, without anything else said on the subject, he looked at me and said, "I sure miss her."

His old blue eyes were so full of hurt and loneliness that I just didn't know what to say. I took a deep breath and turned to look out at the setting sun outlining the row of maples along the street. "We wondered if you'd ever find anybody," I said. "She wasn't with you very long, but she was with you. I guess that's something you can be thankful for."

His voice was so soft I almost didn't hear the whispered "yeah". I turned to shake his hand. "I miss her an awful lot," he said.

You know how sometimes the right words just don't come? If I had it to do over, I'd say, "Clayton, you're my friend. I never met your wife, but I know she was a wonderful lady. And I miss her, too."

Now ol' Zeke likes my coffee. He hobbled in the other mornin' and sat on that stool at the end of the counter like he always does. We were really busy and when Jean came flying by ol' Zeke said, "Coffee, please." A few minutes later he got a chance to ask again. Finally Jean came sailing by and Zeke hollered, "Dammit, I want a cup of coffee!"

Jean stopped. "I'll get your cup of coffee as soon as I can. Don't you have any patience?"

"Patience I got," Zeke howled. "What I don't have is coffee."

I appreciate constructive criticism. Well ... I would if I ever heard any.

"It seems to me," says Luther, "that it must be tough to be an atheist and still do any real long range planning."

"I've got all kinds of customers that come into the store," Tom explains. "There are political conservatives and far left liberals. Some of the conservatives act like they could use a little more fiber in their diets. On the other hand, I sell an awful lot of mirrors to the liberals."

There probably isn't a greater threat to our freedom than a government that wants to take care of us.

Martha writes an article for the local paper once in a while, and she's started working on a cookbook. I freely admit I've swiped a lot of her recipes to use here at the cafe. I'm a pretty decent cook, but Martha's a whole lot better, and we think her cookbook will sell real well.

Anyhow, because of the book, we've gone to some of these writers' conferences. Well, all I can say is that lawyers and politicians sure don't have anything on writers.

You know how you sometimes see a television show or movie with all these people runnin' around tryin' to cut a deal? "I've got a project that is worth millions! All I need is the financial backing. Everybody connected with this will make a fortune!" That kind of thing. Well it's true! There really are people like that. I couldn't believe what I was hearin'.

And talk about lie? At least half those people were talkin' like the printers can't keep the presses runnin' fast enough to keep the adoring public supplied with their books. Everything they write is a hit. If they're to be believed, there won't be a tree left standing in North America before long so we can all enjoy their books.

When they heard about Martha's cookbook, their noses went a little higher than they were already, which put some of 'em on their tiptoes. But I'll bet when the results are all in, she'll have sold more books than a lot of those yahoos who couldn't be bothered when she asked for advice.

Elmer staggered into Jensen's bar last winter and yelled, "It's been a great day! Everybody have a drink! Have one yourself, Jensen!"

Well, Jensen served everyone present and took a drink himself. Then he turned to Elmer and said, "That'll be $24.75."

Elmer put his empty glass on the bar, wiped his chin, and said, "Well, it's been a great day, and I said everybody should have a drink. I didn't say I'd pay for it."

Jensen grabbed him by the belt and collar and gave him the bum's rush. Threw ol' Elmer right out in the street.

Well, after the excitement was over, things settled down for a while. But just as the patrons were starting to talk about other things, the door flew open and Elmer came staggerin' into the room.

"It's been a great day," he yelled. "Everybody have a drink!" Then he turned and pointed across the bar. "None for you though, Jensen," he said, with a shake of his head, "you get mean when you drink."

We were sittin' around shootin' the breeze the other mornin', and all of a sudden we noticed that Pete had gone to sleep. We were havin' a good laugh about it, and Joe said, "It's a sure sign you're gettin' old when you go to sleep while somebody's talkin'."

Pete's eyes popped open and he peered at Joe over his glasses. "No," he said, "it's a sure sign you're gettin' bored. Now if you should go to sleep while you're talkin' ..." And with that he closed his eyes and resumed his nap.

"Y'know how the bus stops at my store before heading into the city?" Tom was sayin' a while back. "Well, they were running a couple of minutes early yesterday, and the bus left just before Mabel Fitch got there. Boy, was she mad! She followed me around the store for half an hour just giving me blue blazes about how she missed the bus, and I should have known she takes the bus every Thursday and held it for her, and on and on. At first, I tried to apologize and calm her down.

Mabel, I said, *you know that bus makes two round trips morning and evening taking folks into town to their jobs or whatever. The last bus of the morning will be here in an hour.*

"She wouldn't let it alone though, so I started stocking shelves while Mabel lit into me. Boy, I didn't think she'd ever run down. She finally eased up, but in a few minutes she got mad all over again. She was really giving it to me when I said, *Mabel, you'll have to repeat that last part. I couldn't hear over the racket.* Well, she started to repeat herself and then stopped.

What racket? she asks.

The racket the bus made when it pulled out just now, I said.

Tom was smiling as he sipped his coffee. "Haven't seen Mabel lately," he said.

Just yesterday Pete was sayin', "I've been comin' across books about outhouses. Books with pictures, books with poems, you name it. The main idea seems to be that it was a great American tradition, and it's a shame they're about all gone."

"Listen," said Joe, "anybody who thinks that is either an idiot or somebody who likes pain."

"Tell me about it," added Luther. "In the middle of winter, in the middle of the night, snow on the ground and twenty below zero -- yeah, it's real romantic to crawl out of bed and take a hike to the outhouse."

"How about in the summer?" Tom asks. "Mosquitoes, yellow jackets, every kind of varmint you can think of and them some. I opened that door one morning and there was a porcupine in there. Ruined my day, I can tell you that.

"We used to keep an old broom in the outhouse," Pete said. "It was for sweepin' around inside the hole. There were black widow spiders in there. The doctors in those days claimed that they treated a lot of people for black widow bites, and a lot of those bites were on folks most tender parts."

"One of life's disappointments," Joe muttered with a shake of his head, "is to be sittin' there lookin' at the catalog and discover that only the slippery pages are left."

"Oh, corn cobs," Pete replied. "The thought brings tears to my eyes and not in fond remembrance, either."

"Say what you like about bugs and critters, winters were the worst," Luther insisted. "As you recall, most of those old outhouses weren't exactly marvels of construction. The wind would whistle through the cracks, and sometimes there'd be two or three inches of snow on the seat. And you can bet some idiot would just up and sit on it instead of sweepin' it off. Everybody who used it after that had a seat rimmed with ice.

"At night, you crawl out of a warm bed and into an old coat. You slide your feet into a cold pair of your dad's old carpet slippers and head

for the door. You open that door and the cold takes your breath away.

"The moon is out, and you can see all right, so you don't bother to light a lantern. What you forget is that since the snowstorm, a lot of trips have been made to the outhouse by folks on the same errand as you, and the snow has been tromped down on the path until it's as slick as calf slobber. Now, it's colder 'n a lawyer's heart, you're still half asleep, and part way down the path you find out why those things on your feet are called slippers.

"Whenever somebody mentions 'outhouse', the only thing that comes to mind is a snow-covered roof, icicles, and my two feet framin' a full moon. I don't want to hear anymore talk on the subject."

How is it that politicians engage in deficit spending as a matter of course, and yet you never see one of them file for bankruptcy? Could it be that they're more careful with their own money than they are with ours? Or could it be they've made enough of our money their money that they don't have to worry about it?

Young Warren Teal is quite a football fan. He was here last Saturday using all kinds of statistics to show why his favorite pro team would win the next day. On Monday, he was back and, as near as I could tell, usin' the same statistics to explain how they got beat 35 to zip.

We were really swamped the other morning and shorthanded to boot. The place was packed when this fella in a suit and tie walks in and takes the last stool at the counter. Right away he starts givin' Jean a hard time about the service, the coffee, the food, and anything else he could bring to mind.

Now I'm workin' the grill, but I can hear what's goin' on. The way I look at it a good waitress is harder to come by than a bad customer, so I was about to give this guy his walkin' papers when I heard him jump Jean's case again.

He was kind of a small guy with a little black moustache that pulled up on one side when he sneered, which is what he was doin' at the time. "I'll bet," he said, as he finished his latest tirade, "that there are times when you really wish you were a man."

"And I'll bet," Jean snapped back, "that there are times you wish the same thing."

Can't say I miss him.

If it does half as much as it could, costs twice as much as it should, and takes four times as long to do it, then it's probably run by the government.

Now you know ol' LeRoy's always been drivin' with his lights on dim anyhow, but the other day he stopped into Tom's store to have a duplicate key made. After the job was done, Tom handed him back both keys and said "let me know if it doesn't work."

LeRoy held up the original key and nodded. "Well, I sure hope it does," he said, "because this one never did."

Antique dealers don't buy antiques. They buy junk. Then they sell antiques.

Gophers like nice, quiet neighborhoods. If the wind blows a lot where you live, you can buy those little pinwheels and stick 'em in the ground here and there. The noise they make when they turn in the wind will often bug 'em enough they'll leave. You can do the same thing with a wooden stake and an old bleach jug. Just cut four panels in the jug, bend 'em out and put the jug over the stake. A tack through the bottom of the jug and into the stake holds it in place.

Martha was in havin' coffee with us the other morning, and she took the opportunity to button hole Tom about a problem.

"Okay, Mr. Hardware Man," she said, "I've got a question. You know our kitchen sink at home with those round metal stopper/strainer things for the drain?"

"Well, sure," nodded Tom. "I'm at your house almost as much as I'm at my own. Alice, I'd guess is there more often than she is at home."

"Well then," Martha continued, "tell me why I can never get that stupid stopper to plug the drain when I want it to. And why is it that when I'm rinsing something, and I don't want the sink plugged, that I always bump the thing by accident and it rolls off the counter into the sink, bounces a couple of times, and lights in the drain dead center? Why is that?"

"Y'know," Joe was sayin' not long ago, "I've seen statues of people, and horses, and dogs, and all kinds of critters, and it occurs to me that there must have been some giants in the sport of pigeon racing, not only the men that bred them, but the birds themselves. Never seen a statue of one, though. Wonder why."

Luther, as you know, is as independent as a hog on ice, and figures he's every bit as good as the next guy -- no matter who the next guy might be. Well, for three days in a row he was pulled over by the same cop and all for what Luther takes to be pretty "picky" little things.

Day one: "No license plate light."

Luther: "So what? Ever'body in the country knows this ol' pickup on sight."

Day two: "License plate obscured by the bumper."

Luther: "Hell, kids on ten speeds are passin' me all the time. Who am I gonna outrun?"

Day three: "License plate still obscured."

Luther: "Oh? How'd you know it was me?"

Both the cop and Luther had been getting more hostile as things went along. After Luther's last comment, the cop said, "Don't get smart with me or you'll regret it."

Luther took a deep breath and stared through the windshield as he let it out with a rush. "Tell me somethin'," he said, turning his head to look at the cop. "What would you do if I was to say you're a fat, arrogant, egotistical, badge-heavy jerk?"

"I'd haul you out of that old rattletrap, snap the cuffs on you and run you in," snarled the cop.

"What if I was to just think it?"

"There's not much I can do about that."

"Okay, then. I'm thinkin' it."

These days you almost never hear anybody say, "A penny for your thoughts." What with inflation and all, what kind of thought are you gonna get for a lousy penny?

Now Ed Wilkins was even more ornery than Zeke, which is sayin' something. But old Ed had a son name of Marion who's been a capable understudy, and he demonstrated at the funeral that he's ready to take over old Ed's duties full time. The services were over and Marion was sayin' goodbye to some of the mourners when he spotted ol' Zeke.

"Zeke," says Marion, "thanks for comin'. Considerin' your age, it must have been quite an effort. By the way, how old are you, anyhow?"

"I'm ninety-one," says Zeke.

"No kiddin'," Marion replies, "it ain't hardly worth the trouble to go home again is it?"

Take a good, long look around Ma Nature's world, and you won't find a fat predator ... until you get to people.

"I have learned to be careful when I use words like 'always' or 'never,' " says Pete. "For example, I once met an army officer who wasn't an egotistical ass."

There's a story goin' around that the only difference between a road kill skunk and a road kill lawyer is that you'll see skid marks in front of the skunk. Well, that's true enough, but what isn't bein' said is that you'll see skid marks on the far side of the lawyer. That's because folks slam on their brakes and back up to make sure they did it right the first time.

"We were in the city the other day," Tom was sayin', "and we went to the mall. Janie came up missing, and we found her in the ladies department of a store checking out the swimwear. She's getting to the age where she really pays attention to that stuff."

He shook his head, made a face, and took a sip of coffee. "In my grandmother's day," he said, "a bathing suit reached clear to a woman's ankles. I took one look at the stuff Janie was interested in and said, *Good Lord, sweetie, you wouldn't wear that, would you?*

Dad! she said, like she was ashamed to be seen talking to such a moron. *This is what everybody's wearing these days.*

Well, I said, *you're not going to wear that. Gee whiz, girl, I'd rather see you wear the laundry instructions tag. It's bigger.*

"She sniffed, stuck her nose in the air, and didn't speak to me again until we got to the donut shop.

"Well, that's me -- Old, Gray, Red-necked, and Evil. Dad the O.G.R.E."

Boy, look at that traffic. When I was a kid, this was a pretty sleepy little town. One time Sam Johnson, our hired man was in an accident right out there. After the car and old Sam's pickup collided, Sam crawled out and found this white-faced city fella sittin' behind the wheel of his car.

"You all right?" Sam asked. The city fella only nodded, so Sam says, "Why don't you get out and walk around a little just to make sure you're okay."

Well the city guy gets out, and he's pretty shaky so Sam kind of leads him around to the door of his pickup. "You look a little shook up,"

Sam says as he reaches under the seat of his truck. He pulls out a brown paper bag and inside is a jug of ol' stumpblower. He takes a quick look around, pulls the cork, and offers it to the city fella. "Here," he says. "A good jolt of this will settle your nerves."

Well, the fella grabs the bottle, takes a long swig, and hands it back to Sam. "Thanks," he says. "I needed that."

Sam corks the bottle and slides it back under the seat. "Aren't you gonna take a drink?" the guy asks.

"Naw," says Sam. "At least not until after the cops have left."

He wasn't all that big, weighing I'd guess no more than fifteen hundred pounds. Yeah, fifteen hundred pounds may be a fair amount for a lot of things, but it's pretty small for a work horse. It's not unusual for one to weigh a ton and a few go a thousand pounds over that. But ol' Bill made up for his lack of weight with horse sense.

He and his partner, Blaze, spent their lives on our place. They were both bays, and Blaze had a white stripe down his face. In winter they pulled a sled or wagon loaded with hay, making a wide circle in the pasture while Dad stood at the back forking feed to the cattle. In

summer they pulled a plow, a mower, a rake, a wagon, or anything else that was needed to get a job done.

I can recall bein' no bigger than a minute and crawlin' under the bellies of those big horses, then tryin' to shinny up those big ol' legs that were like tree trunks to me. Dad would growl at me, not because he was afraid of what ol' Bill and Blaze might do, but because I was gettin' in the way while he was tryin' to harness up. Oh sure, one of 'em might reach down and slobber on my ear or push me with his nose, but neither one of 'em had a mean bone in his body and wouldn't dream of steppin' on a dopey little kid like me.

They were there pulling the wagon when the folks took my brother and me on our first hay ride. There were neighbors and kids from near and far, all singin' and yellin' and havin' a good time. Bill and' Blaze never acted nervous, never even turned a hair when some dummy threw a firecracker from a passing car. Those two old horses pranced along with their heads up and seemed to have a good time right along with the rest of us.

There was a sleigh ride and weenie roast one winter. I remember the songs we sang. When I hear one of those old songs now, I still find myself listening for sleigh bells in the background.

Well, times change and people have to change with them. Dad bought a tractor. He still used the horses some, but then he bought another tractor and another, and pretty soon there wasn't much left for ol' Bill and Blaze to do. On summer days when they would have been working in the fields, now they stood nose-to-tail under the big locust tree in the pasture, dozing in the shade as they switched their tails to keep the flies off.

I remember the fear I felt when a man stopped by the house one day and noticed the work horses out in the pasture.

"You know, Spence," he said, "those horses aren't doin' you any good. Why don't you get rid of 'em?"

Get rid of ol' Bill and Blaze? I thought. Why, they'd always been here. They were as much a part of this place as the house or the barn.

"Work horses ain't worth much anymore," Dad said.

"Well," the man replied, "you could take 'em to the sale yard. You could get somethin' out of 'em for chicken feed or dog food. That's better than payin' for their keep."

"Yeah," Dad said, "I might do that."

But he never did.

I don't recall when ol' Blaze died. I noticed one day that he wasn't there anymore. Nothing was said, but I found a fresh mound of dirt in the small pasture down behind the barn. I knew what it was.

We used a derrick to stack hay. They come in all sizes, but this one was big. The base of it was made of twelve-by-twelve timbers, twenty four feet long. That derrick could put a load thirty feet in the air. It was my job to push the derrick pole and swing it over the stack after a tractor had raised the load.

One day, during the hay season, I noticed ol' Bill standing off to one side with his harness on. I wondered about that. Dad must have brought him there in the morning before we'd done the chores. I walked over to Bill, and he lowered his head so I could scratch around his ears. There was something sad about it. Since Blaze had died, ol' Bill kept pretty much to himself, not having much to do with the saddle horses that ran in the same pasture. I guess nobody could take the place of his old partner.

Anyhow, about midmorning the haystack was as high as the derrick could reach and it had to be moved. A tractor could do it. Ol' Bill and Blaze could do it. But Dad untied ol' Bill and led him over to the derrick.

"He can't do it, Dad," I remember sayin'. "It's too heavy for him."

Dad just looked at me and backed Bill up to one corner of the derrick. He looped a log chain around it, hooked it up and stepped back. "Okay, Bill," he said. Bill stepped forward and took up the slack.

I don't know what I was expecting, maybe a lunge from Bill, maybe Dad yelling, I don't know. But this was somehow more exciting. Ol' Bill leaned into the weight and settled himself into his collar. Slowly those big hooves began to rise and fall like huge pistons as Bill tested the weight. He wasn't trying to pull it, he was only testing. With those hooves still slowly pumping up and down, he shifted to one side and then the other while Dad stood calmly by. Then, somehow, Bill knew just where he had the most advantage, and he lowered that big body and he started to pull.

Those big timbers groaned and shivered, and finally, there was just the tiniest hint of movement -- but Bill sensed it and those big muscles bunched a little more and he stepped into it, turning that fraction of an inch into ten feet in one long pull. But as the corner of the derrick came straight, the advantage was lost.

Dad said, "Okay, Bill."

Bill stopped, heaved one big "whoosh", and turned his head. I suddenly realized both man and horse were looking at me as if to say, "There you are, kid. That's what can be done by a good horse and a man who's smart enough to let him do his job in his own time and in his own way."

And with that they hooked on to the other corner and moved the derrick up to where we could continue stacking hay.

Mom liked to have Dad use ol' Bill to cultivate her vegetable garden because Bill would never step on a plant. She found other things for him to do as well, mostly I think to give him something to do. Like the rest of the family, she considered Bill a part of the place and a part of us.

Ol' Bill is long gone now. A crawler tractor with a dozer blade dug the hole that would be his grave. He rests now, next to his team mate, Blaze, under the soil that they spent their lives working. I don't know about your heaven, but in mine there's plenty of room for faithful dogs and gentle horses.

If you're like me and enjoy grubbing around in the garden, you probably come in with dirt packed under your fingernails. Lately I've started clawing a bar of soft soap before I head out to the garden. With soap under my nails, the dirt can't get in and the soap is a whole lot easier to get out.

Tom and Alice went on a trip to visit

relatives a while back. When they got back, they stopped in for coffee.

"Alice was reading a magazine article to me while I was driving up there," Tom said.

"It was all about how to deal with mean dogs," Alice added.

"So," Tom nodded, as he sipped his coffee, "we pull up to the place, get out, and start toward the house and all of a sudden there's a mean dog. Big, ugly sucker."

"Of course," smiled Alice, "Tom's relatives neglected to warn us about him."

"And the lazy louts didn't bother to come to the window to see who had pulled up," Tom grated.

"So, I told Tom," Alice said, *Remember the article I was reading to you? It said if you stand still and look a mean dog right in the eye, he won't attack you.*"

Tom threw a leg up on the table and jerked up a pant leg, showing off a nice set of tooth marks on his calf. "Too bad she didn't have time to read it to that stupid dog!"

There are honest lawyers, so they say.

I just love sweet cherries. Ever since I can remember I've been crazy about them. One of my first memories is about cherries and my mother.

We had a couple of cherry trees in the back yard and the fruit was at its peak. The best cherries, you know, are way up the tree and clear out at the end of a branch. I had just discovered this for myself and was standing out on a limb that was maybe two inches in diameter at that point. Keeping my balance by hanging on to another skinny branch over my head, I was reaching out toward a big, fat, juicy cherry at the end of a limb and coming up about two inches short. I was trying to decide whether I could lean out a little further and strain just a little more when I heard the "twang" of the spring on the screen door. A couple of seconds later it banged shut, but I was in no position to turn and see who was there.

"Bud! Get down from there before you fall and kill yourself!"

I edged back a little and looked down at my mother twenty feet below as she stood on the back porch with her hands on her hips.

"Aw, ma ...."

"Right now, young man."

My brother and I really enjoyed those cherries. One of us would up with his trusty cap pistol and drill the other guy. The "victim" would grab his chest, yell, and bite down on the

cherry in his mouth, letting the juice dribble from his lips while staggering around in a five minute death scene. Not only did we enjoy this little act, it became twice as much fun when we realized that mom found it really disgusting.

I've got a couple of sweet cherry trees in my back yard today. This last spring we had a bumper crop. I was out in the yard checking them out when I heard the glass door on the patio slide open. I was in no position to see who it was, but then Martha yelled, "Bud! Get down from there before you fall and kill yourself!"

Some things never change.

If you're willing to settle for second best, that's probably what you'll get.

"Remember," Pete was saying, "how in the summer when nobody had ice all the perishable stuff was kept in the spring house?"

"Yeah, and it didn't last long in there, either," Joe replied.

"Us kids all wanted it to hail," Luther grinned. "The folks didn't like it 'cause it could flatten a crop, but if we got enough hail, we could gather up the hailstones and make ice cream."

"My dad ran the local creamery for several

years," I added.

"Oh, the creamery," Luther nodded. "Let me guess. It had a cooler where folks could hang up whatever critters they killed for meat. There was a butcher block and tools to cut it up and lockers to keep it frozen after it was wrapped."

"Right. There was a screened front porch where farmers came by before or after store hours to drop off their milk and cream and picked up clean cans. Nobody ever gave a thought to theft or vandalism."

"The creamery sent out a truck to drop off clean cans and pick up full ones, too. No refrigeration, of course."

"Right again."

"Listen," Tom put in. "You can talk about that stuff, but remember the chocolate milk and orange juice? It came in those little glass milk bottles with cardboard stoppers. Had **five cents** painted in red on the side."

"Oh Lord, the ice cream," Luther sighed. "Nobody gave any thought to fat content in those days. Any kid with a nickel could have a real treat. And for a quarter you could have a big ol' ice cream bar, a bottle of chocolate milk, a bag of salted peanuts and a soft drink with enough left over for a couple of jawbreakers."

"Oh, shut up," Pete groaned. "I'm gettin' a bellyache just listenin' to you."

Cecil and Morton came in a few days ago for lunch. That's kind of unusual, because they don't normally get to stirrin' around before I close at two p.m. Another strange thing was that they both seemed to be about half sober.

They sat down there at the counter and both ordered a sandwich and coffee. I was headin' for the kitchen when Cecil turned to Morton and said, "Now, if you'll just pay me back the money you owe me, I can pay for my sandwich."

"When did I borrow money from you?" Morton frowned.

"Two nights ago. You were drunk at the time."

"Oh, that," nodded Morton. "Well, I paid you back."

"When was that?" Cecil demanded.

"Last night. You were drunk at the time."

"Y'know, we're not just a bunch of hicks settin' around drinkin' coffee," Joe was sayin'. "We're a pretty knowledgeable bunch. For example, we know that the words 'incompetent' and 'incumbent' don't mean the same thing." He nodded to himself, toyed with his cup a minute, then smiled. "Unless, of course, we're talkin' politics, in which case they're interchangeable."

Ever notice that revolutions usually aren't led by fat guys?

There are people around here who get up at the crack of dawn every mornin' and head into the city to join the rat race. Well, that's okay, I guess. They might lead that race for a while, even get a lap or two ahead. But sooner or later, they'll learn what the old timers have always known: In the end, the rats always win.

We watch television just like most folks, and here are these hotshot newscasters who make millions of dollars. The movie and TV stars make just as much or more. If you watch television long enough, you'll see most of 'em give their opinion on the state of things. And, boy, according to them things couldn't get much worse. The answer, of course, is the public needs to donate more money or pay higher taxes so that things can be done to their satisfaction. Now has all that money and fame given them the impression that we really give a hoot what they think? And is it really a progressive attitude or just a guilty conscience?"

After talking it over, we decided it's YES, YES and YES.

Luther doesn't have much time for UFO sightings, conversations with little green men and that kind of thing. We're talking about folks who claim they're abducted by these little critters on a regular basis, and Luther isn't sayin' much when all of a sudden he pipes up and says, "They abduct me every Saturday night."

"Really," Pete nods. "I don't suppose you'd be interested in askin' 'em by for coffee next Saturday?"

"Well that just wouldn't be possible," Luther says, as he shakes his head.

"And why is that?"

Luther straightens in his chair and his voice takes on an indignant tone. "Because, Saturday's our poker night."

"Oh."

Y'know how some people don't like cats and so everywhere they go they've got cats crawlin' all over 'em? Well, I'm that way with lawyers and politicians.

A few days ago, Senator Foghorn showed up with a couple of his aides. He spends most of his time in Washington figuring out ways to spend more of our money, but he shows up once in a while to convince folks to keep payin' him to go back and spend some more.

Anyhow, Senator Foghorn (okay, so his name isn't Foghorn, but I figger it's close enough) and his aides walk in and I say "Foghorn, why don't you and your glow worms go infest some place else? I run a respectable business here and you're givin' the joint a bad name." Foghorn just laughed and headed for a booth.

I happened to be runnin' the cash register when they left, and one of the glow worms (this one happened to be female) steps up and says, "You really should be ashamed of yourself."

I just stood there and looked at her, and pretty soon she started to swell like a toad in fly season. "Well? Aren't you going to ask why?"

"No."

"Then," she sniffs, "I'm going to tell you anyway. You should be ashamed for showing disrepect to such a great man. If it wasn't for men like the Senator, this country wouldn't be what it is today."

"My point exactly," I grinned.

I think I'm gonna have to buy new hinges for my front door.

"I know what the Bible says," Pete nods, "but I have to say I believe in evolution. It goes on all the time. Now you take humans, they're at the top of the chain. Then there's apes, and after that the other warm-blooded animals. From there you go to snakes and lizards and all the other cold-blooded critters. And after that there's the lawyers, car salesmen and politicians."

We were all sittin' around gettin' our morning dose of caffeine the other day when Phillip Shoop walked in and sat down at a table. That's kind of unusual, because this joint ain't high class enough to come up to his normal standards, and to see Phillip up and about before noon is a pretty rare sight.

He started in on Jean, givin' her his order and tellin' her he wanted his breakfast pronto. She pointed to me, sittin' in the corner there with my friends, and told him we didn't officially open until six, and that Bud wouldn't fry a strip of bacon for the Queen before then.

Anyhow, Phillip Shoop was the last of ol' Bert's kids and didn't recall what it was like to be poor. Besides, he was ol' Bert's favorite, and when Bert died, it was Phil who got the ranch. Phil hired all the work done and moved into the city.

Well, when Phil was a kid, he was a snot. Now he's thirty-five years old and just a bigger snot. He insists everyone call him

Phillip, which is why I've always called him Phil.

So, as I was sayin', there's Phil sittin' there bein' obnoxious to Jean, and I was just at the point of walkin' over and tellin' him that I find a good waitress a lot more valuable than a poor customer when Phil puffed himself up and snarled at Jean, sayin', "Do you know who I am?"

Jean just shook her head and said, "No sir, I don't, but I'm sure if you keep on asking around, somebody will probably be able to tell you."

He turned to look at me and opened his mouth, but I said, "Phil, she's right. I don't cook for nobody before six. If that's not good enough, then don't let the door hit you in the butt on the way out."

He shut up and waited 'til six.

Old Sam Johnson used to work on our place, and Sam was quite a character. Whenever things went wrong Sam always said, "Well, nobody's perfect but William Shufelter."

At first we didn't pay much attention to that remark, but after hearing it every so often, we got a little curious. The next time Sam said it, Dad couldn't resist. "So," he asked, "William Shufelter is perfect?"

"The perfect man," Sam nodded.

"And how do you know that?" Dad wanted to know.

"Well, I've never met him myself," Sam admitted, "but I have it on good authority he's the perfect man."

"Well, who is he?"

"My ex-wife's first husband."

"Speaking of the perfect man," Tom nodded, "I've been looking for someone to help out on the cash register and handle the books. I thought I'd found the right person when I asked one guy where he'd learned how to handle money. The guy said 'Yale." Can't do much better than that, I thought. But in the end, I turned him down."

"Why?" Joe wanted to know.

"Well, I asked him his name. He said it was Yorgensen."

In addition to other things, Luther raises pigs. "I don't know how they do it," he was sayin' a while back. "Anytime you want to move a hog from one place to another, his head is, without fail, always on the wrong end."

We were talkin' about tightfisted people the other day, and it wasn't long before Herman Snipe's name came up.

"When I was a kid," Pete said, "there was an old fella name of Mac McArthy lived about fifty miles south of here and him and old Herman favored each other a heap. They were both sharp traders, so tight they squeaked when they walked, and somehow they agreed on a horse trade. About a week after the deal was made, Dad and I happened to be in the store when Ol' Mac an' Herman ran into each other. Boy, they took to callin' each other liars and thieves and both of 'em were claimin' the other guy cheated on the horse trade.

"I recall lookin' over at Dad as we were leavin' and sayin', *If they're both so upset about the deal, why don't they just trade back?*"

Oh, they couldn't do that, Dad said. *They're both afraid they'll get cheated again.*

I was passin' by our combonation city park and zoo the other afternoon. Well, actually it's just a city park now. Somebody ran over the squirrel. Anyhow, I saw ol' Zeke sittin' on the bench. He was kind of hunched forward with his hands folded over his cane and his chin restin' on his hands as he looked up at the sky.

"Zeke, you all right?" I asked.

Zeke gave a little nod at some birds flyin' over.

"I didn't know you were a bird watcher, Zeke."

"I ain't," he rasped, "'cept at my age it's a good idee to make sure they ain't buzzards."

Cecil and Morton used to have a drinkin' buddy named Gene. Now ol' Gene's wife was gettin' awful tired of gettin' along without things because most of Gene's paycheck was goin' for booze. She kept after him to take the cure, and finally he did it.

She made him regular appointments with a psychologist in town and went with him to make sure he got there.

He was in a few months later and I poured him a cup of coffee as he sat on a stool.

"Gene," I said, "I hear you've quit drinkin'."

Gene lifted one side of his mouth in disgust and stared down at the coffee. "Hell's fire," he said, "I had no choice. That damned headshrinker is keepin' me so broke I can't afford to drink."

Moles can be pesky critters. Martha's pretty protective of her roses and finally found something that works - human hair. I just have

Bob down at the barber shop save me the trimmings. He's glad to get rid of 'em. We cut 'em up fine and then spread out a handful about 4 inches down around our roses. Gives the roses extra protein and drives the moles crazy. The hair gets down in their fur. Makes the mole feel the same way I do when Bob lets clippings get down under my shirt collar -- only the mole can't wash it off.

Most folks around here are hard working and practical. They're realists, not dreamers. Well, at least up until the new seed catalogs arrive in the mail.

Well, look at that. It's almost closin' time. Me 'n Martha and Joe 'n Marge are goin' fishin' down on the river this afternoon. Maybe you'd like to come along. 'Course I have to admit that last time out we only hooked two. One was about three inches long and the other one was a little bitty devil. No?

Well, the next time you drop by, your cup will be up there on the shelf with the rest of the regulars. Say, it sure was nice seein' you again. Try to stop in more often, all right? And don't forget to bring along your fishin' pole.